THE ART OF HEALING

You've Turned My Mourning into Dancing

TIWANA TUCKER

ISBN-13: 978-0-692-98295-2

Published 2018 by:
Emissary Enterprises, LLC
Orlando, FL 32837
www.tiwanatucker.com

Photography by Jose F. Rodriguez

Dedicated to my children in heaven:

Caleb, Serenity, and Eden

Until we meet again, ~Love, Mommy

ACKNOWLEDGMENTS

First and foremost, I would like to thank God for this amazing opportunity to share with others the beauty that is birthed out of healing.

To my wonderful, loving, and wise husband, Eddie Tucker, thank you for your unconditional love. Not only have you walked along this journey with me, but you have been my support and inspiration. I am forever grateful for your love, knowledge, and honesty.

To my children Katelyn, Khristopher, Olivia, and Eddie Jr., I am truly blessed to have you in my life. Thank you for your innocence, which reminds me daily that we are God's children and He is a loving Father who wants the best for His own.

To my dear friend Eslin Flynn, thank you for the introduction that changed my life forever. Your courage to share a message that many are not discussing is so needed for our world today. Your gift is appreciated and valued more than you know.

To the leaders of First Steps at the First Life Center for Pregnancy, who are beautiful externally and internally, thank you for your support that was critical to my deliverance. You are a big part of my miracle.

Special thanks to the First Baptist Orlando church for providing a safe haven for women to come and abide for healing and encouragement. I've personally witnessed the transformation of many women who enter the doors of the pregnancy center feeling hopeless and leave transformed with hope. Blessings to such a beautiful ministry!

Contents

PREFACE

Am I the Only One?

Did you know that one out of four unintended pregnancies among American women today end in abortion? In 2014, reports show that 652,639 legally induced abortions took place in the United States according to the Center for Disease Control (CDC) and Prevention Abortion Surveillance (PAS). That's a rate of 12.1 abortions per 1,000 women aged 15 to 44 years and a ratio of 186 abortions per 1,000 live births. It is also a 2 percent decrease from the reported number and a 7 percent decrease from the reported rate of abortions that took place in 2013.

FIGURE 1

2014 Report of Legally Induced Abortions Among Women Groups	
Age Group	% of Reported Abortions
Women 40 years and over	3.6
Women ages 30–39	26.8
Women ages 20–29	58.9
Adolescents ages 15–19	10.4
Adolescents under 15 years	0.3

Within the 2014 rate, women in their twenties account for the majority of reported abortions. Interesting, right? Did you also know that the abortion rates in some other regions, such as Australia, New Zealand, Latin America, Africa, and Asia, have similar abortion rate totals to the United States?

You see, the truth is **you are not alone!** For so many years I personally experienced this lie that often filled me with guilt and fear. Ultimately it isolated me from my family and friends, people who really cared for me. The truth is Jesus came to bring restoration and justice to a fallen world that we all are a part of. It's time to discover the peace that comes with discovering God's truth for your life. It's time to experience the *Art of Healing*.

INTRODUCTION

On a late evening in March 2014, I received a call that changed my life forever. My son's father had attended a ministry conference in Melbourne, Florida, earlier that day and wanted to share with me his encounter with a young lady he had met. The lady had approached him after the service and asked if she could share her testimony with him. She was married with three children, and one year prior, God had healed her from her past abortions through a post-abortive women's Bible study.

I wondered why, since she had gone to him, he was mentioning this to me. He said that he'd had a dream about me and felt I should connect with her. At that time I considered him my best friend and trusted that this wasn't some misconstrued idea. There was some hesitation on my part in the beginning, but I agreed that he could share my email address with her. Within seconds the email went out and I was connected. Not knowing what was about to happen, I awaited the email that would begin the introduction that transformed my life.

The next day, the young lady and I exchanged phone numbers through email and scheduled a time to talk. I felt very awkward when she started asking questions, since I am a private person. She asked me about my abortions that had occurred over fifteen years ago, something I'd never really shared with anyone besides my gynecologist.

Shortly after, she shared her story about how God had transformed her life through attending a Bible study for post-abortive women. I had never heard of anything like this, especially from a biblical perspective. I reached out to the church I had started attending and got connected to a pregnancy center that offered this class.

With numerous questions and much uncertainty, I stepped out in faith and signed up for the class. I realized that this journey was presented to me for a reason, and I didn't want to miss out on what God was doing specifically in this season of my life. Clueless about what the class entailed, I made the commitment to go wherever God would lead me. This just happened to be one of those places.

CHAPTER 1: SEARCHING THE HEART

Psalm 139:23

"Search me, God, and know my heart;

test me and know my anxious thoughts."

My journey of healing began when I surrendered to God all my doubts and fears of going into a new place. This place for me was the post-abortive women's Bible study at a pregnancy center located in Orlando, Florida. I couldn't understand why I was attending a class to learn about God's forgiveness for my abortions when I had already settled in my heart almost fifteen years ago that I was forgiven. I'll never forget asking God, "Why am I here?" I thought if anyone could explain this, it would be the One who created me.

Throughout my journey, I realized that it wasn't only knowing the Father's forgiveness but also experiencing His forgiveness that was needed. I learned that for any journey to be successfully completed, you must be willing to go through all the steps—even when you don't understand why. I learned that for my faith to comprehend the works of the Lord, my intellect had no place in matters of the heart.

The Heart

The heart is one of the most vital organs within the human body. It pumps blood throughout the body and is essential for life. According to the Bible, the heart is so vital that it determines the direction of our lives. Proverbs 4:23 instructs us, "Above all else, guard your heart." In Noah Webster's 1828 dictionary, the word *guard* means "to secure against injury, loss or attack; to protect; to defend; to keep in safety."

Many times when our hearts have been opened to the injustices of the world, our course in life often becomes altered. The good news is that God has made a way for us to get back on course through the redemption He has provided in Jesus Christ.

As I began the post-abortive women's Bible study, the first exercise I was required to do was to search my heart. This was not easy. Over time, I had become insensitive to

2

what others thought of me. I had made a decision early in life to never let anything or anyone get too close. To me this was normal.

Later I discovered that I had been oblivious to the many ways my abortions had affected my life. I was depressed most of the time. I cried at every baby dedication service at my church. I was completely blinded and unconscious of the restrictions I had placed within my life that kept me hostage.

It was God's great grace that brought beautiful women of faith to teach me how to apply God's Word to uncover the devil's deceptiveness in my life that led me to the road of recovery.

The 4 Rs to Recovery

During my journey on the road to recovery, I applied what I call the 4 Rs for searching and revealing the heart. They are:

- **Reflect** on the past.
- Allow unresolved feelings to **resurface.**
- Thank God for **revelation** of the hurts.

- Allow the Word of God to bring **restoration** to your heart.

As I began reflecting on all the images from my past, I realized that this process would give birth to a lot of hidden hurts that I would have to readdress.

During my adolescent years, my father was a major factor in the mental trauma I experienced growing up. He was verbally and physically abusive to my mother, siblings, and me. As I grew in Christ, I realized that there was an evil spirit driving my father's behavior and it was not my father but the enemy who was attacking my life. My hurts and the need of my father's love drove me to a promiscuous lifestyle at the age of eighteen.

While in college, I gave birth to my first child as a single parent. I continued in this relationship and became pregnant four months later with my second child. I was not ready for another child, especially being young and unmarried. I was so afraid and so ashamed. I didn't know what to do, and I panicked.

I reached out to a close friend whom I trusted and who knew all the ropes of having an abortion. She walked me through the entire process, one that I'll never forget.

After having the abortion, I evolved into an overprotective, isolated, strong-spirited woman who was determined to show her independence to the world. Little did I know that when I began declaring my independence to the world I dishonored my dependence on the Father. I'm so thankful for the blood of Jesus.

After reflecting on the past and once the emotions and hidden hurts had resurfaced, I was able to revisit the emotions I felt after having my abortions. Suddenly, it was as if my abortions had just occurred and I was reliving those dark moments where loneliness and regret were all I felt. Although I didn't fully understand what had taken place at the time of the abortions, I was completely aware that they were wrong. I was so ashamed of what I had done that I couldn't share my pain with anyone. I thought I had to deal with it on my own, which was false.

The devil loves replaying old records and accounts in our imagination to stunt our ability to receive the freedom

Christ has made available to us once we accept God's salvation. It is in Christ that we become a new creation, forgiven and set free!

This was such a revelation for me. In fact, Noah Webster's 1828 dictionary definition of revelation is "the act of disclosing to others what was before 'unknown' to them." God is so merciful and gracious! He revealed my pain so that I could experience His love by simply being honest with myself. It was in that moment when I acknowledged my pain and completely surrendered it to God that I experienced the fullness of the Savior.

It was almost sixteen years later that God divinely directed my path to cross the paths of women who could empathize with the pain and struggles of life after having an abortion. With God's Word, my health, my strength, my relationships, and everything I needed for living a godly life were being restored (2 Peter 1:3 NLT). Restoration is the Father's modus operandi!

God's plan is to restore mankind back to Himself. He wants us to be completely healed, delivered, and free from anything that has caused anger, bitterness, depression, shame, guilt, or accusation within our lives. He wants our lives to flourish so that we minister to others the power of the Holy Spirit to overcome the battles of post-abortion. It is only in Christ that we are able to experience this freedom.

Exercise 1: The 4 Rs to Recovery

Take a moment now and find a quiet place to **reflect**. With your eyes closed, ask the Holy Spirit to search your heart concerning your abortion(s) for the next few minutes. When you're ready, answer the following questions:

1. What unresolved feelings **resurfaced**?

2. What hurts did God **reveal**?

3. Now search God's Word concerning the unresolved feelings and hurts to bring **restoration**. Let God's Word do the work in your life. That's what it's designed to do.

CHAPTER 2: DO YOU REMEMBER?

Matthew 7:7 (KJV)

"Ask, and it shall be given you; seek, and ye shall find; knock, and it shall be opened unto you."

I realized that before I could truly deal with the truth about my abortions, I had to resolve certain past issues. I recall being alone in my apartment while my kids were at school and asking God to bring to light all the things that hindered my ability to perceive life in a new way. And trust me, He did just that.

Throughout my journey, the post-abortive recovery class challenged me to communicate with words and journaling what the Father was revealing to me about my past.

I discovered that it was in middle school that my spirit was broken by my father. The verbal abuse I faced during that time attacked not only my self-esteem but also my identity. The physical abuse from my father was just as severe as the verbal abuse. As years passed and I grew older, I learned to fight back. I began defending myself, which no child should ever have to do.

This led me to becoming a very independent individual, making choices that were primarily self-centered. Once I became financially able to move out of my parents' home, God restored my relationship with my father. I was no longer angry with him, but angry at the devil for destroying our bond. I didn't agree with everything my father did, but I learned to respect him so that my days on earth would be long (Ephesians 6:3). Thank God for His great grace.

Renewing the Mind

As a young adult, I struggled with intimacy and most of my relationships without understanding why. The choices I made in my late teens through early twenties were often unhealthy. As I reflected on the reasons I had decided to have an abortion, I realized how fearful I was of being a single parent. I had always said that I'd never be the woman with children who had different last names. I thought that was awful. And yet at the age of twenty-three, I had become the very woman I detested.

After my first child I discovered that my child's father was unfaithful in the relationship. I tried to end the relationship several times, but having a child made it difficult to walk away. I became pregnant with my second child four months after having my daughter and clearly remember being terrified at the thought of becoming a single parent again.

Every single scenario of hardship and pain began to play out in my imagination. I was already a single mom and full-time college student who worked full time. Lacking adequate support from my child's father caused me to burn out fast. Contemplating an abortion was a no-brainer, an easy decision for me at the time. I believed that all my worries of being a single mother with two children would be over once I had an abortion.

Boy, was I wrong! Having an abortion opened up so many unwanted doors in my life, ultimately leading to tremendous regret and low self-esteem issues. For many years after, I struggled with my identity. It was the Father's unconditional love for me that guided me along the way.

The Cycle of Healing

When thinking back to the moment after my first abortion, I began to feel the violation that had taken place within my spirit, soul, and body. In comparison to other painful experiences I've encountered throughout my life, this was like no other. For the most part, it was the regret that ate away at me.

Picture this: there I was parenting a child I had decided to give birth to and at the same time grieving a child I had aborted. Can you image how confused I was without an outlet to discuss my emotions? I was embarrassed to talk to someone at church. I didn't feel comfortable sharing my secret because I knew it was emotionally unacceptable, and it would give a negative reputation to my family's name.

The trauma I faced seemed unforgettable. Physically and emotionally I barely existed. I cried for what seemed like all the time, rarely ate, and was extremely exhausted. Mentally, I was a living train wreck. Not being able to see the face of my child, yet knowing the proof of his existence from an ultrasound photo, was unbearable.

I worked long hours, trying to keep my mind off the abortion. This developed into insomnia, making it difficult to rest at night. I can't express with words the guilt that overcame me every time I looked into my daughter's eyes, knowing I took away a precious life that I would never see in this lifetime.

From the very moment after I had my first abortion, I felt hopeless and continuously cried out to God. I was grieving over my child in secret and was in need of comfort. My soul was restless and the pain was unbearable. Through it all, God, who relentlessly revealed His love for me, often reminded me that I was never alone. In fact, I was so aware of His presence that I felt unworthy to receive such compassion for what I had done.

I realize now God's hand was upon my life. His protection is endless. My personal repentance that brought me to my knees was all God needed. He needed my brokenness so that I could be healed, delivered, and set free. What a loving Father we have. His love never fails.

Exercise 2: Which Hand Is More Evident in Your Life?

In this exercise, you will see how God causes you to triumph in life. Take a moment now and find a quiet place. With your eyes closed, ask the Holy Spirit to reveal the past events in your life. When you're ready, complete the following exercise.

Create a timeline noting memorable events that have occurred in your life. Write the positive events (i.e., fifth birthday party) on top of the timeline. Write the negative events (i.e., parents got divorced at age of nine) underneath the timeline. Once completed, draw a line connecting the positive and negative events together. This will create a zigzag pattern. The line represents God's presence throughout your life. Now notice the hand of God at work in both the positive and negative parts of your life. He has been there and always will be.

CHAPTER 3: THE PROCESS OF PURIFICATION

Psalm 51:10 (KJV)

"Create in me a clean heart, O God;

and renew a right spirit within me."

One night after attending the post-abortive Bible study, I had a dream. I dreamed I was cleaning out a refrigerator filled with a lot of spoiled food in it. As I began throwing the food out, I noticed a perfect loaf of bread on one of the shelves. So I took the bread out to keep it and placed it on top of the refrigerator. I continued cleaning the refrigerator, and the dream ended.

The same day I asked the Holy Spirit to give me understanding of the dream. The interpretation came, and it was so clear. The refrigerator was a representation of my heart, and within my heart remained many unclean things that had been there for a long time. I'm talking years!

However, also within my heart was Jesus, the "bread of life." And yes, He is still perfect today! I thought, wow, such an awesome picture of how the Father sees my heart. I knew right away that it was time to begin dealing with the "old things" God was exposing. There was no use for hiding those painful memories anymore, especially since they were being revealed. It was time I dealt with the matters of the heart.

Forgiveness

Experiencing God's forgiveness is part of the purification process. On my journey of healing, forgiving others who were involved in my decision to have my abortions wasn't hard for me to do. It was forgiving myself that was difficult. I was very hard on myself and was my own worst critic. For most of my adult life I was unhappy and used my accomplishments in life to overcome the feeling.

I created rules and barriers for protecting myself from experiencing pain, or so I thought. After my second abortion, I had no expectations from the men I chose to date. Being in a non-committed relationship was my choice because I didn't want to be responsible to anyone. I continued in this way until I met my son's father, and then we dated for several years before I had my second live birth.

Our relationship suffered because of the distrust I had for men. As parents, we raised our child together easily as our values and beliefs were the same. As friends, his companionship meant everything to me because I knew he truly cared for me. But outside of these two roles, it was difficult to see him as a husband because of my blindness. I created isolating barriers around my children and myself.

Nevertheless, if someone had asked me if I knew I was forgiven, I would have answered yes, because God's Word says I am. I was taught that forgiving others is not for their sake but also for mine. Fifteen years later I truly began to experience God's forgiveness.

The Scripture that literally changed my perception was Isaiah 43:25. God says, "I, even I, am he who blots out your transgressions, for my own sake, and remembers your sins no more." I read that Scripture while attending the post-abortive women's Bible study and thought, how amazing that God canceled my faults and offenses not for my sake but for His. This wasn't based on whether I deserved to be forgiven, but because where sin abounds, God's grace abounds much more (Romans 5:20).

Then it began. All the pain I had never shown began flowing out of me like a waterfall. My eyes filled with tears of joy that could not be expressed with words. The Father revealed His love for me, which is unconditional and unwavering. Oh, how sweet it is to be loved by Him!

Purification

According to the Levitical law, an unclean person was cut off from the sanctuary and the festivals. *Easton's Bible Dictionary* defines purification as the process by which an unclean person was restored to the enjoyment of all the privileges of the sanctuary and the festivals.

Immediately after I experienced God's forgiveness, a cleansing began to take place within me. God began to purify me from all the conflicting emotions that were created as a result of my past abortions. 1 John 1:9 says, "If we confess our sins, he is faithful and just and will forgive us our sins and purify us from all unrighteousness."

God restored many years of my life, and I began valuing it in such a beautiful way. I desired things I thought I never would, like being married or taking tennis lessons. All the empty spaces in my life that were formed out of fear were now noticeable. I was no longer afraid to fill those voids in my life. I was on a journey to discover what the fillers were. That's when I started enjoying life to the fullest.

Exercise 3: Purification

Take a moment now and find a quiet place. With your eyes closed, ask the Father to purify you from all the uncleanliness created as a result of your past abortion(s). When you're ready, answer the following questions:

1. What are some things that I enjoy?
2. Where are some places that I would like to go?
3. What hobbies do I like?

God wants you to be free to experience the abundant life. He wants to restore every part of you so that you are enjoying all His privileges in life.

CHAPTER 4: REJECTION AND THE NEED TO DISCOVER LOVE

1 Corinthians 13:4-5

"Love is patient, love is kind. It does not envy, it does not boast, it is not proud. It does not dishonor others, it is not self-seeking, it is not easily angered, it keeps no record of wrongs."

One of the most difficult issues I've encountered in life was keeping the secrets of my abortions from my family. I was ashamed that I had not one or two, but three abortions before the age of thirty. I remember the moment I shared with my mom my first abortion.

I was twenty-three years old when I had my first abortion. I was living at home with my parents and had become extremely ill afterwards. I hadn't planned to tell my mom, but because I was in excruciating pain, I had no other choice but to ask my mom for help. Not to mention that all the ibuprofen in the world wouldn't have helped with the agony I was experiencing.

The look of disappointment in her eyes was heartbreaking. It was so intense that I could not stop the tears from falling. I was in a state of shock because of the physical and emotional trauma I had just experienced. On one hand there was relief that I wasn't pregnant anymore, but on the other hand there remained the pain of being violated. Fear quickly affected me, and for a while I couldn't hear anything from God because deep down inside I knew what I had done was a violation to Him.

Learning God's Truths

God's Word says that He knew us while we were each in our mother's womb and He knows every hair on our head. God knew of my abortions before they ever occurred. But through His unconditional love and mercy, He has made a way for forgiveness to anyone who needs it.

Removing the weight of my sin allowed me to live a life of purpose. For a long time, I experienced signs of depression and wasn't even aware of it. The result of depression controlled how I reacted to people and special moments in my life. My body, soul, and spirit had been infected with guilt, shame, and fear. The symptoms I experienced for years after my abortions were:

- Guilt
- Shame
- Emotional numbness
- Low self-esteem
- Lethargy/prolonged sleeping patterns
- Isolation from others
- Crying during baby dedication services at church
- Overprotectiveness of my children
- Workaholism

Other symptoms of depression that can affect the body, soul, and spirit are:

Body:

- Sterility
- Miscarriages
- Eating disorders
- Drug and alcohol abuse
- Increase in crying
- Loss of patience

Soul:

- Regret

- Nightmares

- Exhaustion/tiredness

- Promiscuity

Spirit:

- Fear of God

- Sadness during specific days (i.e., Mother's Day, anniversary date of the abortion procedure)

- Grief

The post-abortive women's Bible study helped me realize that God had provided a Savior for this very reason. To transfer the weight of my error, I had to bring all of my past issues that were buried deep within my heart and release them to the Father. Once I released them, I was then able to receive God's words of truth for my life that are rooted in love, joy, and peace in the Holy Spirit.

Now that I had completed the process of purification, the next step was to replace the "old food" within my heart with God's truth! It was critical that I saw the old food exactly as it was, rotten and useless. None of it added value to my life, but instead occupied space that should be filled with useful memories that were healthy for my body. God created uniqueness in everyone, and there are some critical things that are exclusive only for your design.

My Life's Leading Roles: Defining the 5 Ws

The technique I'm about to share is something every child learns in elementary school—the 5 Ws: who, what, when, where, and why. When someone writes a story, these components are necessary for telling the entire story. In the table below, I've used the 5 Ws to create a structure for defining my leading roles in life.

MY LIFE'S LEADING ROLES				
Who am I?	What do I do?	When?	Where?	Why?
Wife	Support, pray, care, encourage, love, believe, respect, submit, refer to my husband	Forever	Everywhere	Honor and love for God and my husband
Mother	Meet the needs of my children, provide unconditional love, pray for them, and direct their paths	Forever	Everywhere	I love taking care of the needs of my kids.
Organizer	Put things in order	All the time	Writing, planning, cleaning at home, conversing	Helps me to see the "big" picture
Worshipper	Dance before the Lord	Music is playing	Bedroom, living room, recently in worship service	I fall in love imagining that I am in a room full of angels, dancing in the presence of the King! Best slow dance ever.

FIGURE 2. Sample of My Life's Leading Roles

After completing the table, I connected each row and column to form sentences. An example of this is as follows:

- As a wife, I support, pray for, care for, encourage, love, believe in, respect, submit to, and refer to my husband because I honor and love God and him forever.

- As a mother, I meet the needs of my children by providing unconditional love, praying for them, and directing their paths because I love caring for them all the time.

- As an organizer, I put things in order because it helps me to see the "big" picture through writing, planning, cleaning, and conversing all the time.

- As a worshipper, I dance before the Lord while imagining I am in a room full of angels dancing in His presence, mostly at home while playing music.

As you can see, I was able to put together affirmations of truth pertaining to the roles in my life that God has given me.

Exercise 4: Life's Leading Roles

Take a moment now and find a quiet place. With your eyes closed, ask the Holy Spirit to help you see yourself the way God sees you. When you're ready, complete the following exercise:

On a sheet of paper, create a table and complete each of the sections using the below as a guide. Remember to be honest with yourself.

MY LIFE'S LEADING ROLES				
Who am I?	What do I do?	When? (how often)	Where? (online, office, home, etc.)	Why?

CHAPTER 5: THE IMPRINT OF TRANSGRESSION

Isaiah 43:25

"I, even I, am he who blots out your transgressions, for my own sake, and remembers your sins no more."

Throughout my life, I often reflected on the what-ifs from my past abortions. The dreams of what my life would have been like if I had not aborted my children would never become a reality for me. Those memories were engraved—or "imprinted"—within my soul, causing barriers that resulted in isolation.

During one of my Bible study sessions, the Holy Spirit taught me the difference between sin and transgression. I learned that sin is an act and transgression is the result of that act. The perfect picture revealed to me by the Holy Spirit was so simple. Imagine walking along a muddy path that has never been stepped on. The shoe in this example represents the sin or act that was committed. Once the shoe is pressed into the mud, it leaves an imprint, or the result of that act. The sin can be removed from the path easily by lifting the shoe; however, the imprint doesn't go away on its own.

To remove the imprint you will need a supernatural experience to occur, like rain that changes the form of the mud, leaving no sign that the sin occurred. The rain in this example represents the Holy Spirit, who has been given by the Father to the believer in Christ. He wants to remove all the imprints from your heart.

God Has Blotted Out Our Transgressions

For a long time, I didn't know how to express God's goodness in this area of my life. I knew of His mercy because I was alive to tell this story, but I didn't understand how having an abortion was redeemable in the eyes of God, or furthermore, a testimony to the church. I was raised in an apostolic church for most of my life and never felt comfortable enough to talk about sex, much less having an abortion.

Now that I was experiencing the Father's love and mercy through His Word, I saw the Father's love for me. In Isaiah 43:25 God says, "I, even I, am he who blots out your transgressions, for my own sake, and remembers your sins no more." Until I read this verse at the post-abortive women's Bible study, I couldn't recall hearing the revelation of that particular Scripture so clearly. The Father was saying to me that because He has blotted out my transgressions, there would never ever be another record of it again and since He can't recall it, why should I?

His love is everlasting, and He provides for our success in this lifetime. Jesus is our daily provision. He was bruised for our transgressions so that we can encounter healing whenever we need it. The Father wants us to experience Him more than what the world would try to offer us. His love never fails!

Ask for the Rain

The Father loves to communicate with His children just as any parent does. In fact, when my children don't quite understand something, they simply ask. God has given us the Holy Spirit to be our helper. Within the post-abortive women's Bible study, this truth became more evident to me. The Bible says that the Father gives seed to the sower and that the sower sows the Word. It was with the Word that I was able to defeat all of the devil's lies. In prayer I uprooted seeds of bitterness, guilt, shame, and anger, and sowed seeds of love, freedom, peace, and joy. I refused to carry around symptoms that were no longer a part of my life.

I needed the Holy Spirit to comfort me and guide me into all truths. It was amazing to watch how the Lord began watering the seeds I sowed within and allowed others to witness this transformation in my life. I'll never forget how gracious God was to me in that season.

Exercise 5: Removing the Imprint

Take a moment now and find a quiet place. With your eyes closed, ask the Holy Spirit to be your teacher. He is ready to aid you through your journey of healing. When you're ready, answer the following questions:

1. What engraved memories do I want God to remove?

2. What seeds do I need to uproot on my journey of healing?

3. What seeds do I need to sow on my journey of healing?

"Rain is only important for people who have seed in the ground." – Unknown

CHAPTER 6: REMOVING THE BLIND SPOTS

Genesis 3:6–10 (KJV)

And when the woman saw that the tree was good for food, and that it was pleasant to the eyes, and a tree to be desired to make one wise, she took of the fruit thereof, and did eat, and gave also unto her husband with her; and he did eat. And the eyes of them both were opened, and they knew that they were naked; and they sewed fig leaves together, and made themselves aprons. **[Shame]** And they heard the voice of the LORD God walking in the garden in the cool of the day: and Adam and his wife hid themselves from the presence of the LORD God amongst the trees of the garden. **[Guilt]** And the LORD God called unto Adam, and said unto him, Where art thou? And he said, I heard thy voice in the garden, and I was afraid, because I was naked; and I hid myself. **[Fear]**

Acknowledging the inner pain (even long after the physical pain) of having an abortion is a battle for most post-abortive women. In most abortive cases, the pain that these women experience indicates shame or weakness. The fact is every woman experiences pain; however, each level of it varies.

I thought avoiding the pain after my abortions was the best way of coping with the emptiness I felt. I became emotionally numb to the thought of being in any relationship. The borders around my heart were so thick, it was impossible to penetrate them.

It wasn't until I started attending the post-abortive women's Bible study that I had the ability to go beyond those barriers I had created. I was able to confess the pain I experienced and how it had prevented me for years from seeing myself the way God saw me. Giving voice to my uncertainties, failures, and disappointments allowed me to understand that I am human and in life everyone experiences pain. The good news is that God wants us to be of good courage, for He has overcome the world! It wasn't until I began sharing my experience of shame and regret for not having my children that I was able to properly mourn.

Seeing through the Eyes of Jesus

A saying of one of my favorite pastors is, "You don't see with your eyes; you see through them." The truth is that you see with your mind through forms of pictures. Every image has an emotion that has a meaning attached to it, and likewise, every emotion has an image that has a meaning attached to it.

My mind literally became a constant battlefield that I wasn't sure I was victorious over after the abortions. The images from the surgical procedure and the actual pain I experienced played continuously like a movie within my mind. For a moment I'd experience immediate relief, but that lasted only for a little while. Sorrow instantly filled my heart each time I unconsciously reflected on the images of my abortions. I no longer viewed the world the same since then.

I clearly recall declining the anesthesia that was offered for the pain before each abortion procedure. I thought that if I were to die having an abortion, I would do it with my eyes wide open. That sounds insane, but I truly lost all hope during those moments.

While on the surgical table, I literally felt the pain of my womb being ripped out of my body. Because of the decision I made, I was being violated. Despite all the facts given for having an abortion, I was truly unprepared for what would occur after the procedure.

When I realized that I couldn't change what had taken place, my perception on life became completely distorted. I would love to tell you that after my first traumatic experience that I never had another abortion, but that's not the truth. I underwent two more procedures, and it wasn't until the third one that I experienced an awaking within me. I cried out to God and made a vow to Him while lying on the surgical table. With all my heart, I vowed that if He allowed me to live through this, I would never have another abortion in my life. And from that day forward, I have kept my promise to the Father!

I got pregnant with my son about a year later and married the father of my child years after that. That was nine years ago, and since then the Word of God has continued transforming my life. I am a loving wife and mother, and understanding the picture the Father has for me keeps me well balanced. Through the Word I was able to replace the feelings of guilt and defeat in my life with the help of God's mercy and grace. As I grew closer to Jesus, I began to understand the grace of God that is sufficient for my life.

New Garments

As a woman, I believe clothing often defines our femininity in the world. Colossians 3:12 in *The Message* says, "So, chosen by God for this new life of love, dress in the wardrobe God picked out for you: compassion, kindness, humility, quiet strength, discipline."

Throughout my journey of healing, I slowly began taking off the covering of sin and guilt and putting on the robe of righteousness. At times when I felt heavy and burdened, I learned to put on the garment of praise and take off the spirit of heaviness.

Also throughout my journey, I developed a battle plan to use when the enemy tried to accuse me of my past life. My plan consisted of praise and worship. Through praise I was able to gain strength from the Lord for the things I could not naturally obtain on my own. Through worship I could renew my mind and gain God's perspective about my future. I gradually began moving past my feelings and accepting the freedom that awaited me.

According to Isaiah 61:3, we are "oaks of righteousness, a planting of the LORD for the display of his splendor." With the robe of righteousness, I learned to understand that God saw me just like He saw His Son, full of love and grace. There was no escaping this love. Just as Jesus was in the world, so am I.

Exercise 6: Re-clothe Yourself

Take a moment now and find a quiet place. With your eyes closed, take a minute and reflect on the fact that the Lord wants to make you a display of His splendor. You will need your Bible to complete the following steps:

1. In your Bible, do a word search on *love* and *righteousness*, and read the passages in context and make note of God's heart toward His children.

2. In your quiet place with God, write Him a letter. In this letter, pour out and confess to God how you see yourself. What do you despise or dislike about yourself?

3. Now finish the letter by asking God, "How do You see me after all I've written?"

To become a display of splendor, you must be willing to take off some things. When you're ready, complete the following statement.

Prayer: "Father, I, [*say your name*], take off fear, shame, and guilt today. I now put on the robe of righteousness that the Father freely gives me because of Jesus. I choose to clothe myself in compassion, kindness, humility, quiet strength, and discipline to become a planting of the Lord for the display of His splendor. In Jesus's name, amen!"

CHAPTER 7: THE CAST

Psalm 55:22

"Cast your cares on the LORD, and he will sustain you;

he will never let the righteous be shaken."

The Art of Casting

I learned about a valuable tool called casting while on my journey of healing. In Psalm 55:22 we are told to cast our cares on the Lord and He will sustain us. In this text, the word *cast* means "to impose; to bestow; or to rest," which is a command from the Lord. When I finally decided to act on this command, I began to let go of all the pain caused from my abortions. The moment I decided to cast my cares on Him, the Lord immediately released healing and peace over me, and I wept like a little child.

I literally felt a heavy weight being lifted as I poured out to the Lord in tears. I didn't understand this until later, but I had reached a fork in the road on this journey that required me to make a decision about my pain. I had to choose whether I would continue to hold onto memories of the hurt and shame from my abortions or to create new memories of redemption and forgiveness.

This moment was about being vulnerable and transparent, which didn't come naturally for me. For years I cried secretly by myself and encountered several instances where everything in my life was at a standstill. Once I released all the pain that was embedded in my heart to the Father, He began pouring His love into those empty spaces.

This is the part where I discovered the meaning of true repentance on my journey. I surrendered to the Lord, placing all my worries and insecurities into His loving care. Today, brothers and sisters, please know and trust that God will make all things new, turn what is evil into good, and finish the good work He started in you. It is the love of the Father that covers a multitude of sin.

Trusting in the Lord

The Bible tells us to "trust in the LORD with all your heart; do not depend on your own understanding. Seek his will in all you do, and he will show you which path to take"

(Proverbs 3:5–6 NLT). On my journey of healing, I was faced with the question that we all ask ourselves: Do I trust God? In my mind, I said yes, but my lifestyle didn't display a child who totally trusts her Father with her life.

I had to reexamine my motives in life and how every choice that I made without consulting the Father wasn't wise. Each day I began to make a conscious decision to inquire of the Lord and trust that He would answer. I further determined to release my heart into the hands of the One who holds my future. I no longer carried the burdens associated from my past abortions, which was liberating.

For most of my life I had absolutely no clue that I was carrying around heaviness in my heart. One day the Lord revealed to me what carrying heaviness looked like. He impressed upon me that it's like having dirty laundry around the house. If we are not consistent with washing our clothes, our laundry baskets will begin to pile up and become very smelly and heavy. Each time we add more clothes to the basket, the clothes on top get buried deeper toward the bottom.

Our baskets can only become empty when we decide to clean the dirty laundry. That's exactly what occurred when I released my pain to the Lord. He created in me a clean heart, and he renewed a right and steadfast spirit within me (Psalm 51:10).

Beautiful Exchange

God is so amazing! I learned that deliverance is an actual experience and is available to believers who are willing to biblically follow God in faith to receive it. Everyone's journey to healing in this area will look different; however, knowledge and awareness are the first steps that open the door to healing. It becomes a conversion within the heart, from what seems impossible to becoming the possible.

The more I learned about God's character, the more I could trust Him. It was getting His perspective that was key to me knowing what He truly thought about me. God says, "For my thoughts are not your thoughts, neither are your ways my ways" (Isaiah 55:8). In the Bible Jesus is described as the pathway to life. He is the redemption plan for mankind and has redeemed us from sin, poverty, sickness, and death.

This beautiful transformation within my heart transpired when I decided to entrust my unborn children to the Lord and inquire of Him and His heart concerning their lives. I am now confident that one day my family will be reunited because of this very simple but profound act. When we let go and allow the Holy Spirit to usher in the presence of the Lord, all fear is removed from our lives. What a glorious day it will be when I will see my children in heaven just as I see my living children. Up until this point in my life I never fully understood what being completely forgiven looked like. Now I truly understand, for whom the Son set free is free indeed (John 8:36)!

Exercise 7: Cast Your Cares

Take a moment now and find a quiet place. With your eyes wide open, see your cares about having an abortion and present them to the Lord. In your Bible, do a word search on *trust* and *fear,* and read the passages in context and make note of God's heart toward His children. The next time that you visit the memory of your abortion, remember to cast your cares and let God make this a peaceful moment for you and your loved ones. Add your name to the prayer below and make it your personal confession to the Lord.

Prayer: "Father, I, [*say your name*], cast the guilt and shame from my abortion(s) on You for I know You will take care of me. Thank You for the beautiful exchange that only You can provide: giving me beauty for ashes, the oil of joy for mourning, and the garment of praise for the spirit of heaviness. In Jesus's name, amen!"

CHAPTER 8: NEW BEGINNINGS

Proverbs 10:7 (KJV)

"The memory of the just is blessed: but the name of the wicked shall rot."

Months prior to relocating to Florida with my family, I had a dream that was surreal. I dreamed that I was pregnant and having labor pains. In the dream, I called my mother and asked her to take me to the hospital. When she arrived, it was dark outside as I walked out of my apartment building to get into her car. The hospital's emergency room just so happened to be at the end of the same block as my apartment building.

As I walked into the emergency room, I told the nurse that I was about to have my baby. The nurse asked me to complete some forms, and while she was handing me the forms, my water broke. As I looked down I saw that I had given birth and the umbilical cord was still attached to the baby.

I remember my baby's face so clearly. She had a beautiful chocolate complexion with big brown eyes and thick curly black hair. I couldn't take my eyes off her. She was the most beautiful baby girl I've ever seen. I remember asking myself, who was this beautiful baby who left such an impression on my heart? Then before I knew it, the nurse clipped the umbilical cord right where I was standing and gave me a cloth pad to prevent the leakage.

When I woke up, I immediately shared the dream with my husband. At that time neither of us knew what to think. Three years later while sitting in a post-abortive women's Bible study, the Holy Spirit brought the dream back to my remembrance. It became so clear to me who this baby was and why I was so impressed by her beauty.

That night while I was lying in bed, the daughter whom my husband and I aborted almost ten years before visited me as an infant in a dream. She was awakening in me the justice that needed to occur to move forward in life. God wanted to deal with what is dear to His heart: **life**. He reminded me that He is the giver of life and that He will never change, no matter what has occurred in our lives.

Blood Speaks

Part of the post-abortive women's Bible study consisted of allowing yourself time to mourn the loss of your child or children. This was not an easy process, and I can't imagine going through it alone. The women at the pregnancy center created a safe haven for me. They became my friends who not only walked with me but also prayed with me when I couldn't pray on my own.

As my eyes were being awakened to the beauty and the mysteries of life, the Holy Spirit began revealing truths concerning the Father's heart. My husband shared a powerful word the Lord had given him during this time. He said the Lord revealed to him that when there has been an unjust act of bloodshed in the land, the blood of that person cries out, invoking justice to be demonstrated publicly.

I thought, Wow! This is so true for the lives of children who have been aborted. This unjust act didn't involve them in the decision-making process. It only involved the emotions or concerns of the women and men included in the act. When my husband and I realized this truth, we understood the importance of honoring our children publicly.

This included seeking and asking the Father who our children were and what He calls them. The Bible tells us that Adam named everything in the earth. It wasn't until Adam assigned a name to the person, place, or thing that value was added. We were open to hearing the voice of the Lord for the identity of our children, and trust me, He answered.

Thanks be to our Lord for His grace and unending mercy that allowed us to bring justice and honor to our children.

> **Eden**—Place of delight or pleasure (Zephaniah 3:17)
> **Serenity**—Tranquility, peace, clear, calm (John 14:27)
> **Caleb**—Whole, all of heart (Numbers 13:30)

A Time to Mourn

When my husband and I began properly mourning our unborn children, our lives changed completely. We were given the opportunity to publicly mourn our children. While preparing for that day, I cried the entire morning. During the car ride, my head hung low while tears continuously ran down my cheeks. I remember glancing at the color of the sky, which was gray and cloudy.

As we walked through the doors of the chapel, my heart became so overwhelmed. I was in awe at all the thoughtful details that were taken into consideration for honoring my beloved children. There was one white rose for each of my children with a blue or pink ribbon indicating their gender, which was simply beautiful. At that moment, I acknowledged the life of my children and was awakened to the reality that their spirits are alive.

Beloved, our heavenly Father knows that our future includes our families being reunited once again. No one is lost or left behind when you make the decision to trust the One who is the creator of all living things!

Honoring Our Children

In Psalm 127:3 (NLT), the Bible clearly states, "Children are a gift from the Lord." When we honor our abortive children, we are declaring justice for the unjust act we created. I never knew the importance of this act until I experienced it. The Day of Honor service at the Bible study marked a point in time that was taken from my children's lives and redeemed it. On June 5, 2014, I dedicated my children's lives to the Lord. I announced openly that I entrusted their lives completely to the One who knows them better than I do. I admitted how sorry I was for not being brave enough to have them and how, if I could turn back the hands of time, I would make a different choice. The Father knew of my children before they were formed in my womb and has set them apart. What an awesome picture!

Exercise 8: Get Connected!

There are so many ways that you can give honor to your child or children who are in heaven. Below are some examples I have been a part of or have witnessed:

- Write a letter in memory of your love for them.
- Compose a song or poem in their honor.
- Release a balloon as a symbol of letting go.
- Plant a rose bush in their honor.

I encourage you to take this very first step by contacting someone to help you begin your journey today.

For more information or to find a recovery group near

you, please contact:

International Helpline for Abortion Recovery
1-866-482-LIFE (5433)
24/7 Confidential Care
www.internationalhelpline.org

CHAPTER 9: BUILDING AN ALTAR

Exodus 17:15

"Moses built an altar and called it The LORD is my Banner."

After the post-abortive women's Bible study ended, the Lord began speaking to me about building an altar within my home. My first thought was that this was an ancient practice of the Old Testament that really didn't pertain to me because of Jesus. But it was actually the opposite. The Holy Spirit began teaching me the importance of the blood of Christ and the need for the remission of sin. There were issues within my heart being revealed concerning my life that would have been impossible to see had I not received healing from my past abortions. God was creating in me a clean heart and renewing a right spirit within me.

My closet became my altar and meeting place with the Lord. When I needed a quiet place away from my children and the everyday minutiae of life, I would go in my closet and sit down before the Lord. It was at the feet of Jesus that I could continue to place my troubles down no matter how light or heavy they were. In exchange, I came out refreshed, restored, and revived. For the believer, we have Jesus, who is the ultimate sacrifice for us. Through His body and His blood we are redeemed.

Communion Is the Answer

Communing with the Lord daily was a significant part to my peace of mind. I rested often for moments throughout the day, quieting my mind, body, and soul to hear from the Lord. Often I would take a walk outside or ride my bike, or sit quietly on my balcony with a cup of coffee, or find a bench in a nearby park and soak in the sun and listen to the sounds of birds. Each time, the Father talked to me in such a beautiful way.

I noticed the different types of trees and their uniqueness for what they produced. When I read my Bible, I saw words that I'd seen many times before completely different. I also saw my prayers answered instantly.

One day the kids and I were at our community pool, and my son got hungry and wanted pizza. At that time we didn't have any extra spending money, so I told him, "Let's tell the Lord." So we stopped and asked the Lord for pizza and thanked Him for providing it.

As we were leaving the pool area, we stopped inside our leasing office for water. While getting water from the cooler, one of the office staff members walked up to us and handed me a resident appreciation gift that included a free large pizza and soda certificate. We were in awe of how fast God answered our prayers. I thought to myself, what a great way to share with my children how God wants them to have all their hearts' desires, even pizza!

In His Presence

God transformed my life by turning my mourning into dancing literally! One evening while attending a prophetic worship service with my husband, I met a woman who had brought the most beautiful flags with her. Throughout the service she waved her flags and danced before the Lord. It was absolutely beautiful. At the time I had no reference for the flags, but I knew there was something special about dancing before the Lord.

I asked her if I could try one of her flags, and she gave me a pair of rainbow flags that represented the grace of God and His covenant. As I began dancing before the Lord with the flags, I felt this sweet peace overcoming me. I knew I was in the presence of the Father and all his angels were dancing with me. I felt so alive and free that I couldn't stop dancing.

I found so much pleasure dancing before the King and waving a banner of grace in His honor before His people. I was so caught up in that moment that I no longer saw the people. I simply enjoyed the presence of God that entire night.

After the service, the woman who had given me the flags came to me. She stated that God's presence was all over me and that this was my calling from the Lord. Since that day, I've been worshipping the Lord in dance and spiritual warfare. I've found an inexhaustible peace in declaring God's love in dancing prophetically over His people, His church, and His land.

Exercise 9: Building Your Altar

Take a moment now and find a quiet place. With your eyes closed, ask the Holy Spirit to give you a vision for building an "altar" where you can commune with the Father. Once you have an idea, write it down below.

_____

_____

_____

_____

_____

_____

_____

_____

_____

_____

_____

_____

_____

CHAPTER 10: DELIVERANCE IS YOURS

2 Corinthians 3:17

"Now the Lord is the Spirit, and where the Spirit of the Lord is, there is freedom."

The previous chapters in this book contain testimonies of challenges and victories I've faced throughout my life as a result of my past abortions. Now it is your turn to experience God's amazing healing power in your life. You may be asking yourself, Why me? Well, for starters, you are reading this book, which is no coincidence! I and so many other women and men are living witnesses of God's transforming grace given to those who seek Him with all their heart, soul, and mind. I believe His unfailing love is drawing you to Himself for such a time as this.

God is merciful, and He is waiting for you with open arms no matter what you've done. It doesn't matter what your background or culture may be, or where you are right now in the world. The truth is God wants you to be free from the spiritual and physical weight of sin caused from having an abortion. His anointing will take away our burdens and destroy the yoke of bondage from our lives (Isaiah 10:27 KJV).

My sincerest desire is that you'll allow the Father to heal you from the inside out, removing all that has bound you for so many days, months, or even years. As you enter your personal journey of healing, remember that your willingness and obedience are required. Once you are awakened to the redemptive plan of Christ, all fear is removed. From this day forward, may you never see yourself as a victim in this area again. You are *victorious*!

The Art of Healing

The art of healing is God's creative power that delivers us out of darkness and brings us into His marvelous light. From the beginning we were made in His image and His likeness. Today, His Word remains throughout His creation and it is also for our unborn children. Their lives are not abstract memories, but beautiful portraits designed by God.

As you begin your personal journey of healing, start trusting in the Lord and not your own understanding. God has a specific picture of your unborn child that He wants to reveal to you and that will change your life forever. As you begin to acknowledge the fear, shame, and guilt from your past abortions, the Lord will in exchange redefine those painful memories by replacing them with new ones. Your heart will literally become a blank canvas that He begins drawing upon. The dark, hurtful memories of your abortion will be transformed into honorable memories that you can enjoy.

Imagine the fine details and the extra care taken as He paints the perfect image of your child upon your heart. Each memory He creates has a unique brush and a special color palette. There is even a special brushstroke that is used to bring variation and intensive depth to His work. Talk about being fearfully and wonderfully made!

Getting to Know the Father

Before the post-abortive Bible study, I thought I had the right to make the decision of having an abortion. After all, it was my body and God gave us the ability to make choices. I never took into consideration that thinking this way was totally selfish. When I realized this, that's when the Holy Spirit taught me the goodness of God's mercy.

Yes, it was my body and I did have a choice, but in that moment I didn't choose life; I chose death. God's Word clearly tells us to choose life and that He is the giver of it! As women, we have been entrusted with the gift of bearing children into this world. Our wombs were created to provide the physical space for the care and nurture needed to create a child.

He has also equipped us with the ability to provide for our children after giving birth. Our bodies miraculously produce milk that includes the nutrients to sustain their lives. When we begin to take the time to appreciate this mystery, we will be open to the beauty of bearing children for the glory of God. You see, family is God's idea, not man's. We've been adopted into His family along with our unborn children. It is through our families that all the nations of the earth are blessed.

CHAPTER 11: SHARING THE LOVE OF JESUS

Matthew 5:16 (KJV)

"Let your light so shine before men, that they may see your good works, and glorify your Father which is in heaven."

After being healed from my past abortions, I knew that I must share this good news with other women and men who have also chosen to have an abortion in their lifetime. Through this liberating yet painful journey, I could see Jesus and discover God's plan for redemption. It brings my heart great joy knowing that one day my children in heaven and my family on earth will all be together. We must share this truth within our families, communities, and most of all, our churches.

I learned from the post-abortive women's Bible study how to search deep within my heart and allow the Father to heal everything I was carrying because of my ignorance and pride. I was able to nail all of the pain, guilt, and shame that had been buried for over fifteen years to the cross where Jesus has paid for it all. And in exchange, I found freedom in learning that I am free not because of my actions, but because Jesus has redeemed my life. He has made a way for every woman and man to encounter healing that brings hope and restoration to our spirit, body, and soul through the work of the cross.

Transformed and Unashamed

When I attended high school in the nineties, I was first introduced to Planned Parenthood at my high school's health clinic. They offered free contraceptives and lots of information for the prevention of teen pregnancies. Because these services were so easily available, many of my friends and I thought we were doing the right thing by using their services. This included talking about family planning, birth control methods, and, if needed, abortion services. Sadly, as a teenager I, along with my peers, followed the counsel given by this organization and made some unfortunate mistakes early on in life.

Today I am free and unashamed to share my testimony with the world. My abortions were my choice, and God knew if I continued in this way I would be led to self-destruction.

As I began to take responsibility for my actions, God saw my heart and forgave me. He revealed my future as it relates to my family and gave me hope. The good news is that other women and men who are hurting because of their decision to have an abortion can be free too!

God's agenda embraces the world. There are no secrets with Him. As creator of all things, He knows our hearts' intentions, including the answer to the pain we all experience when we choose to be silent about our abortions. I learned throughout my journey that the more honest I was with myself, the more honest I could be with others. I didn't have to deny my feelings or experiences; I simply had to trust in the Holy Spirit to use me as a witness. What a great reward it is to see women and men be healed for the kingdom of God!

There Are No Losses in the Kingdom of God, Only Gains!

The same year that I was healed from my past abortions was the year that I began walking with other women who were seeking healing from their abortions. I began building relationships with women of all ages to start a journey that would forever change their lives. Every time I was introduced to someone stepping out on this journey, my heart was overwhelmed with excitement for the joy that was set before them because of their commitment to the path.

It filled my heart with exceeding gladness to witness and join them on their journey that the Father so mercifully had set them upon. Witnessing God's truth working in the lives of the women who desperately sought Him satisfied my soul. I was truly amazed how God used these same women to later become vessels of living testimony to draw others into His goodness. No matter what age the women were, I realized that the story never changes: We that are lost become found and awakened to God's plan to redeem and restore us back to Him. Every time we decide to be a witness for the kingdom of God, all of heaven celebrates the life that will be forever changed because of Jesus! He is the way, the truth, and the life (John 14:6 KJV)!

CHAPTER 12: THE CAUSE

John 10:10 (KJV)

"The thief cometh not, but for to steal, and to kill, and to destroy: I am come that they might have life, and that they might have it more abundantly."

It's Not about Us—It's about the Cause!

For those who are reading this book, I pray that you begin to understand that life is a gift from God. Our world exists because God created male and female and commanded them to multiply and replenish the earth. Families exist to replicate and reproduce God's very nature in the earth. Deuteronomy 30:19 says:

> "This day I call the heavens and the earth as witnesses against you that I have set before you life and death, blessings and curses. Now choose life, so that you and your children may live."

We must begin to understand that this is a heart issue and it matters to God. Let's not become insensitive to the life-giving qualities He has so graciously given to us. Our children deserve a chance to live. It is imperative that the Gospel of forgiveness and grace is made known to those who have never heard it before. If you know someone today who is pregnant and contemplating having an abortion or has had an abortion, I urge you to share this resource with them. God desires to heal them from the inside out, no matter what condition they are in. All He asks is that we come just as we are.

Technology Social Reform

Technology gives people the opportunity to reach others globally within seconds. We can share information faster electronically than we can physically. It's time to join together and target our forthcoming generations with the skills and resources that will give them a hope and a future. It is our moral responsibility to educate and provide them with tools that are easily accessible and available through various social platforms.

Every time we choose laws that degrade women and men by stripping away their God-given rights and abilities, we come into agreement with those who promote these ideas.

Help bring change to this world by sharing this good news today with someone you know.

TESTIMONIALS

Be encouraged, be refreshed, and be strengthened. ~Tiwana Tucker

WALLS BEING TORN DOWN

Joanna's life had many ups and downs. At a young age she was raped by her mom's boyfriend. She later ran away from home and got involved in selling drugs and guns with other family members. She dropped out of high school and aborted her first child when she was seventeen years old. Now in her late forties, she had been introduced to a post-abortive Bible study for women. During one of the study sessions, while sharing her story, she paused and explained to the group that she was having a hard time remembering the details of her abortion. For a long time, her abortion was one of many disappointments buried deep down inside, along with other tragedies in her life.

Joanna returned to the next class with tears in her eyes. She stated that she had asked God to help her remember her baby as we had instructed her in class, and God did just that. She realized that in fear she had built a barrier around her heart and it was time to destroy it!

SING, O BARREN WOMAN – TAMMY'S TESTIMONY

Isaiah 54 was the Scripture promise given to my husband and me. We were both Christians and we loved the Lord and each other very much. However, I always struggled with the first verse of Isaiah 54 and questioned God. It says, "Sing, barren woman, you who never bore a child; burst into song, shout for joy, you who were never in labor." In 1973, I became pregnant and had an abortion. When God gave me this Scripture, I was not sure if He wanted me to be glad about not having a child. I was so confused about it, for thirty-eight years to be exact. But today it makes sense, because in 1977 when I accepted Jesus Christ, I was forgiven of my sins, and God no longer saw my pregnancy nor my abortion. To Him, I was a barren woman!

LET GO AND LET GOD

On a Saturday afternoon at the post-abortive Bible study group, Tonya took a bold step and decided to share with the group an ultrasound photo of her aborted child. She had recently completed a class on forgiveness, and shortly after, the Holy Spirit began speaking to her.

With tears in her eyes, she reached into her wallet and took out an ultrasound photo of her aborted baby that she had been carrying around for three years. This was her secret that she often would gaze upon that no one knew of except the father of the aborted child. Tonya decided in that moment that it was time to properly mourn her unborn child. With tears we prayed, and she dedicated her baby to the Lord.

REFERENCES

American Dictionary of the English Language. Noah Webster. 1828. http://webstersdictionary1828.com/Dictionary/abridge.

Easton's Bible Dictionary. M. G. Easton. http://eastonsbibledictionary.org/3024-Purification.php.

Jatlaoui, T.C., A. Ewing, M. G. Mandel, et al. *Abortion Surveillance*— United States, 2013. MMWR Surveill Summ 2016; 65 (No. SS-12):1–44. DOI: http://dx.doi.org/10.15585/mmwr.ss6512a1.

Jatlaoui, T. C., J. Shah, M. G. Mandel, et al. *Abortion Surveillance*— United States, 2014. MMWR Surveill Summ 2017; 66 (No. SS-24):1–48. DOI: http://dx.doi.org/10.15585/mmwr.ss6624a1.

RECOMMENDED RESOURCES

1. Burke, Kevin. *Redeeming A Father's Heart: Men Share Powerful Stories of Abortion Loss and Recovery.*

2. Harris, Cathy. *Created to Live: Becoming the Answer for an Abortion-Free Community.*

3. Kennedy, Lynn Kennedy and Myrtzie Levell. *First Steps: A Journey of Healing to Abortion Recovery.*

4. Levell, Myrtzie. *Journey of Healing: Finding Healing and Hope After Abortion.*

BIBLE STUDIES FOR ABORTION RECOVERY

First Life Center Pregnancy

First Steps to Abortion Recovery

3125 Bruton Blvd., Suite B

Orlando, FL 32805

407-514-4520

Email: Info@FirstStepsJourneytoHealing.com

International Helpline for Abortion Recovery

1-866-482-LIFE (5433)

24/7 Confidential Care

www.internationalhelpline.org

www.ingramcontent.com/pod-product-compliance
Lightning Source LLC
Chambersburg PA
CBHW031522040426
42445CB00009B/360